Tattoo Aftercare

The Full-Guide For The Freshly Inked

WRITTEN BY RYAN JAUNZEMIS

FOREWORD BY ALBERT ALCARAZ A.K.A. TAT THAT ASS

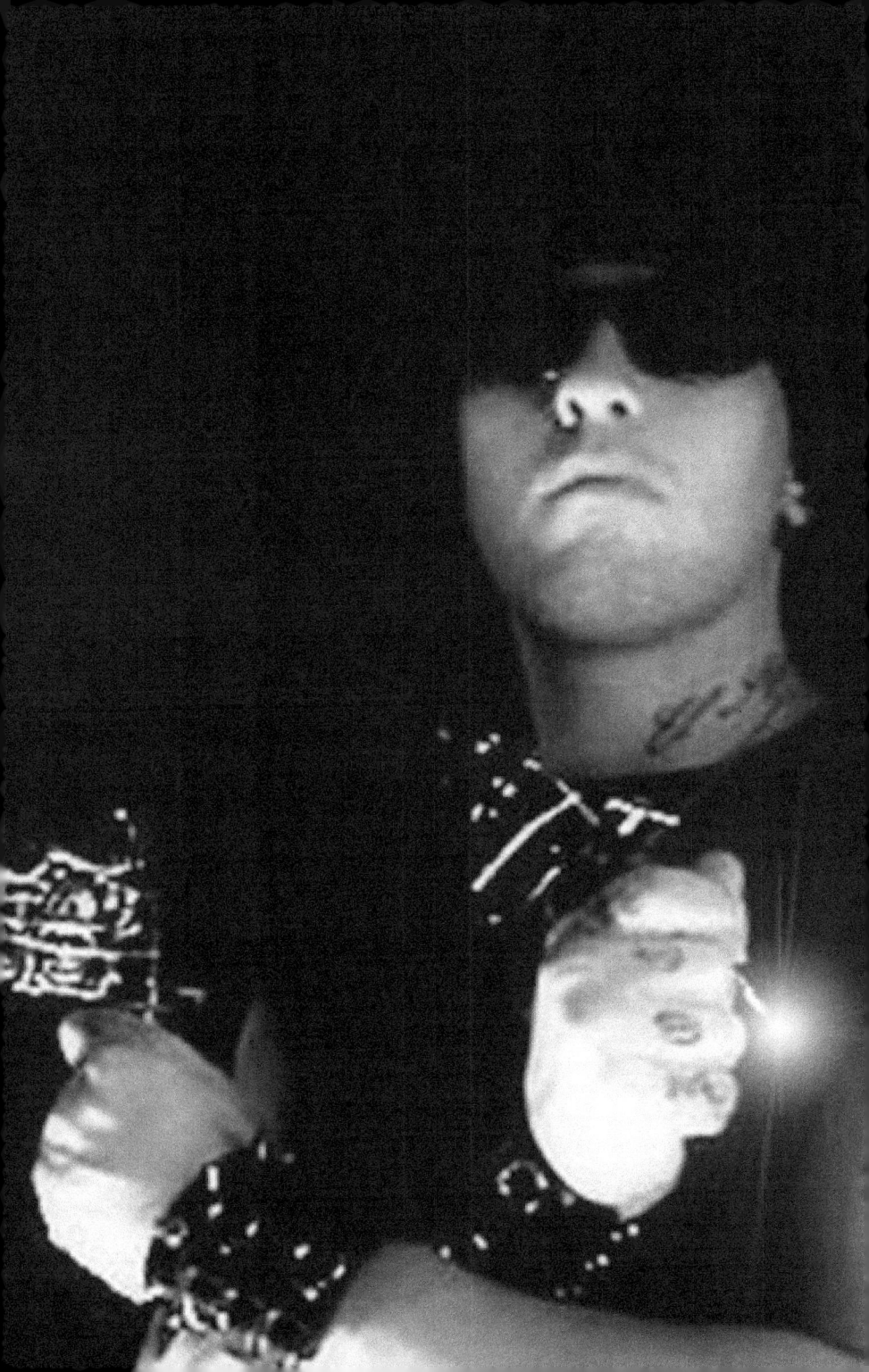

Tattoo Aftercare

The Full-Guide For The Freshly Inked

WRITTEN BY RYAN JAUNZEMIS

FOREWORD BY ALBERT ALCARAZ A.K.A. TAT THAT ASS

Disclaimer

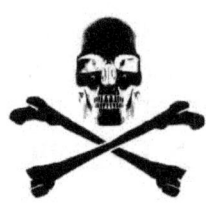

THE AUTHOR OF THIS BOOK (RYAN JAUNZEMIS) DOES NOT ASSUME ANY LIABILITY FOR YOUR PERSONAL ACTIONS.

The advice on "**TATTOO AFTERCARE**" in which I am going to deliver to you here within the pages/confines of this book **CANNOT** be taken for **ANY** sound medical advice, and **MUST** be taken **FOR ENTERTAINMENT PURPOSES ONLY!**

If **YOU THE READER** so choose to partake in **ANY** of the following advice or activities discussed or suggested here within then you do so **AT YOUR OWN RISK!**

Upon reading this article, if you so choose to partake in any of the activities so mentioned then you agree to waive the right to sue Ryan Jaunzemis, **AND ANY OTHER APPLICABLE PARTIES** in the event of any injury, death, or any other incidental or consequential damages arising from your actions. You also agree to assume and accept all risks of serious bodily injury arising from such activities.

Furthermore, **I AM NOT A DOCTOR OR A PHYSICIAN**. Any such medical advice that is given here within, are reports of **MY OWN PERSONAL FINDINGS AND EXPERIENCE**, and is advice that **I MYSELF** have used during the natural healing process of my own tattoos; in which I have found most beneficial to **MY OWN** personal success, health, and well-being. Any such advice given **MUST** be taken solely **FOR ENTERTAINMENT PURPOSES ONLY**, and **AT YOUR OWN RISK!**

If **YOU THE READER** so choose to partake in **ANY** of the advice given here within then **YOU THE PARTICIPANT AGREES TO TAKE FULL RESPONSIBILITY FOR THEMSELVES, AND FOR THEIR ACTIONS!**

*Remember: Before using any such advice, always remember to first consult your doctor or physician.

Foreword

BY ALBERT ALCARAZ
A.K.A. TAT THAT ASS

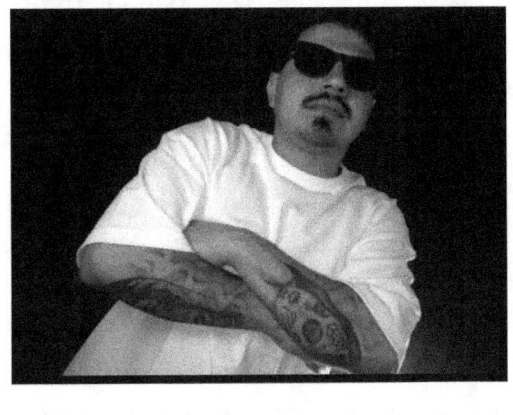

As soon as I met Ryan we were both eager to show each other our own styles of tattooing. Half-way through our first session our personalities and mindsets clicked together on our visions of business, money, ink, and women. From that point on, I had quickly recognized the fact that Ryan and I were slowly becoming good friends—possibly even business partners.

I've been tattooing for over 20+ years; from working in shops, to tattooing out of the house, and even while in jail using nothing but pencil-graphite and a single staple.

Ryan and I have done 100s of hours of work on each other, as well as several collaborations with numerous other artists. Now, almost 4-years later, it's a lot more than just tattooing; as we both have many other means of generating income.

Personally I fuck with only REAL people, and Ryan is a BOSS! That is why I keep him in my inner circle. He is sharp-minded, intelligent, and knows how to translate his hustle into many different forms of income; books, music, CDs, DVDs, etc.

Ryan's new book "**TATTOO AFTERCARE**—*The Full-Guide For The Freshly Inked*" is his step-by-step guide to preserving your fresh ink (Your artist will appreciate you respecting his work).

This book has some amazing advice in it, but what's even MORE amazing, is the fact that THIS book (Unlike so many others that have been written about this subject) is not written from the perspective of a doctor/lawyer. This book is actually written by a REAL MUTHA FUCKA from the streets who ACTUALLY DOES TATS HIMSELF and HAS TATS ON HIM; meaning that THIS book has been written in a language that I believe anyone who is involved within our industry will EASILY be able to read, and really understand. It doesn't matter whether you've just gotten your first tattoo or you're an experienced veteran, or even if you're a fellow tattoo artist with years-of-experience under your belt, this book is for YOU!

After reading Ryan's book(s), and then viewing things from his unique perspective, one can clearly see why Ryan's specialized knowledge and expertise are very essential factors in the works of my business.

Not many people can do what Ryan has done; incorporating the street hustle, AND the business aspect.

When you listen to Ryan's music, watch his music videos on his *YouTube* channel, and read his various publications, you will quickly recognize that he is about this lifestyle FOR REAL. His tats tell a story; from the struggle, to the hustle, to the executive position where he now sits—comfortably.

In this book Ryan is going to share with you some of his wisdom and knowledge that he has experienced throughout life, as well as his experience "Under the tattoo gun."

Ryan has well-over 200+ hours of ink work on him—I know, because I did most of it. He has gone through what works and what doesn't work, so he knows the best way to take good care of a bad-ass tattoo.

*Remember: Having the artist do the work is only HALF of the tattoo. The OTHER PART is up to YOU!

Thank you for reading. If you have any questions, comments, concerns, etc. please don't hesitate to contact me, and don't forget to TAT THAT ASS!

Thank you, and get your ink on!

Albert Alcaraz

Albert Alcaraz A.K.A. Tat That Ass
702.834.0768
Tat.That.Ass8340768@gmail.com

Dedication

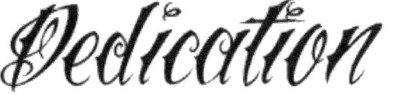

To *my homeboy Anthony,*

Thank you for having the trust and confidence in me to place a fuckin' needle in my hand—knowin' I ain't ever even tattooed before—and allowed me to just go HAM on dat azz like it ain't no thang. Guess it'z like that old sayin' goes, "Cocaine is a Hell of a drug!" Anywayz, that first experience has really opened my eyes to a new found niche that otherwise I may have never found within myself—good shit homie!

Thank you, & much love,

Ryan Jaunzemis

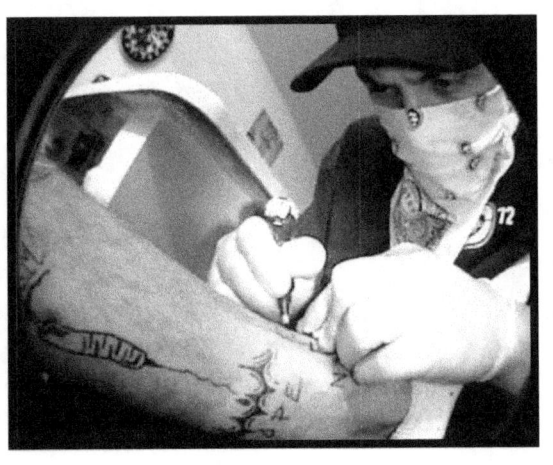

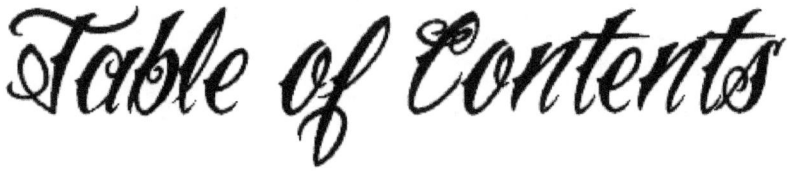

Table of Contents

Prologue

#WTF IS ON MY SHEETS?

Huh… What IS that? I thought to myself as I lay in bed.

I had awoken quite abruptly. I'd felt something odd against the left-side of my face; a cold and slimy-like sensation.

What the fuck?

It was as if I was lying in a puddle of something wet, but it was up near my cheek.

Hmmm…

I propped myself up—slowly squinting my eyes, as it was still quite early in the morning.

Eww…

"What the fuck is THAT!?" I said to myself out loud as I sat up quickly.

As I was sitting up in the middle of my bed I quickly turned around to stare back down at my pillow.

"Arrgghh FUCK!" I exclaimed.

Instantly I'd noticed what had appeared to be a GIANT wad of *A&D Original Ointment* that had apparently smeared off of my new tattoo that I had just gotten the night before on my left shoulder.

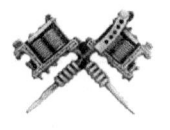

I was out-and-about with my buddy Bryan Agee, screwing off over in Hollywood; hanging out, shotgunning beers, and chain-smoking cigarettes on the Sunset Strip—our typical weekend soirée. I was 18 at the time, but I would have some of my older friends buy us beer. Bryan and I would go out and get piss-drunk while blasting the stereo and cruising around aimlessly up-and-down the strip in his old black throwback *Oldsmobile*. We enjoyed chillin' out on Friday and Saturday nights before usually making a quick cameo-appearance at *The Palace* (A famous local night club off of Sunset and Vine) to dance around, listen to music, and try to pick-up on random young hotties.

On THIS particular evening, Bryan had suggested that the two of us visit the *Shamrock Social-Club* and finally get OUR FIRST TATTOOS—we had been talking about doing so for ages.

Bryan and I had met back in the 7th grade. The two of us had been going on-and-on about getting tattoos ALL THROUGH HIGH SCHOOL—we were just waiting until we FINALLY turned 18 (Due to California law—BOO!). I had been rapping and making music ever since I was 8-years-old, and had always dreamed of getting all "*Sleeved up*" so that I could rap on stage with my shirt off, and represent the west coast to the fullest!

"Hey Jaunzemis! I got a few extra bones man, let's get some ink done tonight!" Bryan suggested.

"Yeah, it's fuckin' time man!" I replied.

"I know right!? We been talkin' about it for like… WHAT? Like YEARS now? Ha ha!" Bryan said.

"Hell yeah!" I exclaimed, "Let's do it brutha!"

On this particular evening the moment just seemed right, so we hopped onto the 101 North (The Hollywood Freeway) and went for it!

Bryan had decided that he wanted to get a tiger tattooed on his shoulder ("Tiger" was his pet-name—a name given to him by a girl named Katy that he was seeing at the time), and I (Being a pro skater/Soaper) had decided that I wanted to get the company logo for *Relate Video Productions* (One of the companies that I was sponsored by at the time). The *Relate*-logo was a small tribal-like looking symbol; two separate hook-like shapes connecting to one-and-other forming the letter "R" in the middle—I couldn't wait to finally get it done. I was really excited!

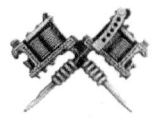

While Bryan was getting his tiger tattoo done, I was on the other side of the tattoo parlor getting my *Relate* tat worked on. I had instructed the artist to color in my tattoo using a bright royal-blue ink with a silver-outline.

Now, one would THINK that someone who worked in a professional shop would know what the fuck he/she was doing. But, little did I know at the time, my "Artist" was really just in fact, an apprentice—**lesson learned: NEVER take things at FACE VALUE; especially in the world of tattooing!**

The artist, to whom I had <u>ASSUMED</u> would have had a greater level of expertise (***2nd lesson learned: NEVER ASSUME!**), had COMPLETELY fucked up my tat! The stencil was fucked up, the outline of the tattoo was jagged, a few of his *lines were blown out*, but worst of all, the advice that this tattoo "Artist" had given me on the aftercare/afterlife of my tattoo was COMPLETELY off base! In all honesty, I think the guy might have even been drunk!

Anyways, my artist, upon the completion of his work, smeared on a GIANT goopy glob of *A&D Original Ointment* (Without even rubbing it in), and then wrapped up the fresh tattoo in *Saran*-wrapping (*Cling film*). He then instructed me to: 1, not shower afterwards, and 2, to just take off the wrap when I got home and quote-on-quote, "Just smear on a lot more ointment before bed, and continue putting it on every day for like two weeks or so."

I listened to my artist's advice, but being the fact that I was a complete noob to the world of tattooing, I had quickly made the mistake of taking this "Advice" as ABSOLUTE DOCTRINE (As most newbies will tend to do)—whoops!

Upon leaving the shop, Bryan and I drove down to the store; where we each purchased 3 GIANT TUBES of *A&D Original*

Ointment— enough that we thought should last each of us for the entire two weeks (And then some).

This should be enough, I thought to myself.

Still to this day, I wonder to myself: *HOW IN THE FUCK DID THIS IDIOT EVEN MANAGE TO GET A JOB IN A *PROFESSIONAL* SHOP?*

I mean seriously, for 1, this asshole couldn't tattoo for SHIT, and 2, he DEFINITELY didn't know JACK SHIT about tattoo aftercare for his customers. In no way what-so-ever was this "Professional", and in all honesty I was rather pissed.

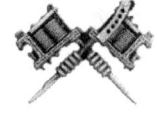

Hmmm... I thought.

"So much for my fuckin' pillow I guess"—I was speaking to myself out loud.

As I was sitting up on my bed staring back down at my pillow—admits the giant goopy smear of ointment—was the bright blue mirror-image of the *Relate* logo INKED into my pillow! It appeared as if the ointment had sucked most of the ink RIGHT OUT OF MY SKIN and had transferred it into the casing of my pillow. But, there was more.

I began slowly crawling my way out of bed. It was early, and I was still quite groggy for that time of the morning—I've never really been a morning person, fuck all THAT shit! But, while I was getting up, I looked down and noticed a bit MORE blue ink on my sheets.

"WHAT THE FUCK!?" I said to myself.

It appeared as if EVERY AREA on the bed where I had rolled—i.e. EVERY SPOT where my shoulder had been laying throughout the night—some of the ink had bled out and had transferred onto my sheets. The same image (Though mirrored and in reverse) was repeating itself over-and-over-AND-OVER AGAIN—in bright blue smears ALL OVER MY SHEETS!

Wow! Oh well, fuck it!

I knew my sheets were stained and ruined for life- (No, not the types of stains that you jerk-offs were thinking of... You sick fucks! ;) -and I felt as if something just wasn't adding up.

Maybe this guy doesn't really know what he's talking about. I wonder...

I had assumed that SOME of the ointment was obviously going to rub off throughout the night. I figured that I'd have to wash my sheets later on, but that was to be expected—no big deal. I never expected that it would actually pull out some of the fresh ink! I had thought the ink was SET in there—like over! Done! Finished! Permanent! End of story! But... I guess not.

At the time, I didn't understand the simple science behind a tattoo's natural healing process. I didn't understand that by applying all of that excess ointment, combined with the fact that the tattoo was covered, and also combined with the fact that you sweat while you sleep (Which causes your pores to open up), along with TONS of other variables (Which we will discuss later), that any type of predicament such as this could have ever happened.

Yo man fuck this shit! I'm gonna call that fuckin' shop an ask um what tha fuck iz up.

I phoned the tattoo parlor in Hollywood later that afternoon and asked for the manager; so as to enquire him about a few of my concerns. The manager of the shop informed me, that the person who did my tattoo was the quote-on-quote "New guy", and that he was still "Just learning"; to which he quickly apologized for.

Thanks for mentioning that shit… JACK ASS!

The manager of the shop—a MUCH more experienced tattoo artist—then began giving me COMPLETELY DIFFERENT advice on tattoo aftercare; to which I quickly applied! Later, my tattoo—for what it was—had healed up rather nicely, and without infection. There was a bit of color/pigment loss, but the shop manager agreed that he would do some free touch-up work for me later on (After the healing process was fully complete).

Fine, whatever! It is what it is.

The main lesson that I'm trying to teach you here, is that with just a little bit of knowledge—CORRECT KNOWLEDGE— one can save themselves a TON of problems; especially in the world of tattooing! I mean really! No one wants to have to sit in traffic, to drive from El Segundo, all the way out to fuckin' Hollywood (Which can take like an hour-and-a-half or so;

depending on traffic—L.A. traffic is a bitch) just because some fuck-tard didn't know what the fuck they were doing!

Don't just assume that just because someone quote-on-quote "Does tattoos", that THAT PERSON actually knows what the fuck he/she is actually doing.

The bottom line: **<u>LISTEN TO THE PROFESSIONALS</u>**!

Section 1

AFTERCARE

And… Voilà! Beautiful! Here we are, the FINAL stages of your new masterpiece!

Now, I know you're excited. But I want to warn you, that if you don't apply the PROPER aftercare-techniques to your tattoo, then your new bright and beautiful master<u>piece</u> might just go… all to… *pieces.* <u>Pun</u>ny, right? ;)

Okay, for real though… All jokes aside, congratulations! YOU did it! YOU thought of an idea. YOU got up off of the couch. And YOU made it happen! And now, here you are; leaving the shop with that brand-new tattoo that you've been thinking and talking about getting for so long. Your idea has FINALLY come into fruition! It's real. It's physical. It's tangible. You can hear it, smell it, see it, taste it, and touch it. It's there for life! But, if you want to really preserve your fresh ink so that it will stand the test-of-time, and stay bright, vibrant, & colorful, then we're going to have to sit down and discuss a few technical details (Fun stuff, I know. But trust me, it's worth it!)

Now, as you've probably noticed ALREADY, there are literally tons and TONS of people out there, running their mouths and trying to give YOU advice.

First-things-first! I would recommend that you follow MY advice and not your "Friend's" advice (Who probably only has three tattoos).

After many, MANY YEARS of experience in the field of tattooing (Along with the fact that I now have over 60+ tattoos MYSELF; at the time of writing) you can be WELL-ASSURED that I myself have BEEN THROUGH the natural step-by-step healing process on NUMEROUS OCCASIONS, and have seen it all before. I believe that you will find the information, in which I am going to be presenting to you here, VERY enlightening, VERY beneficial, and to which I myself believe will definitely aid and assist you in the natural healing process of your new tattoo.

My goal here, is to give you THE BEST advice that I can. While YOUR GOAL here, should be to FOLLOW THIS ADVICE to the best of your abilities. Because really, why would you want to spend all of this money—sometimes up to several hundred, and possibly even several THOUSAND dollars—on a tattoo that just ends up peeling and flaking away. All because you were either 1, ignorant of what to do (Which is not your fault; as no one has ever taught you this information before—this is not a subject that is taught in school) or 2, because you simply just got lazy, and didn't want to take the extra few-minutes out of your day so as to apply the PROPER aftercare procedures.

Now, a tattoo NORMALLY takes anywhere from between 2-weeks to a month (And sometimes even up to a month-and-a-half) to FULLY heal; depending upon the type of tattoo, style, size, and/or placement.

So what does this mean to you? It means, that you're going to have to do certain things during this 2 to possibly 6-week time period if you want your tattoo to heal PROPERLY (I.e., without scabbing up, without losing any of its color/pigment, and without infection, etc.). But hey, don't worry fellas. It's <u>not</u> that difficult! In fact, the simple process in which I'm going to reveal to you here—along with the extra tips & techniques that I'm going to talk with you about—are all really quite easy to follow and implement; once you really begin to understand the big picture.

TIME TO "WRAP" IT UP!

Typically, after the completion of a new tattoo, your artist will *"Wipe the tattoo down"* with an interesting smelling green-liquid known as *"Green Soap."* The artist will then apply a very thin layer of *Vaseline* or an anti-bacterial ointment (Such as *A&D Original Ointment*; or something similar along those lines), and will then, simply bandage it up.

Depending upon the size of the tattoo, this may be done with a simple gauze-bandage, or multiple bandages and medical tape. Every artist has their own method, but this is BY FAR the most common.

I lived in Northern England for a year (My X-wife is British) and this "Wrapping" method was done there in shops as well. I also have other friends from around the globe—who have all confirmed to me—that this is a typical procedure for shops in their areas as well. It may possibly be an OSHA regulation (Or something to that extent) but I don't know for certain (Nor do I really care). It does seem to be a universal procedure, but in actuality your tattoo doesn't need to be wrapped up after its completion. And personally, I've found it to be more of a hassle than anything!

Now, MOST PEOPLE want to rip the bandage off right away, as everyone (Especially the younger crowd) tends to get super excited, because they want to take tons-and-tons of selfies for their Facebook/Instagram, etc. Technically, you should wait AT LEAST a few hours or so. But, as mentioned before: You don't really HAVE to. You can take the wrap off right away if you want to! The only reason why I would recommend keeping the wrap on, is that it will help to protect your damaged/traumatized skin, and it will stop the lymphatic fluid and blood/plasma from continuing to flow. When a wrap is applied over the tattoo, these fluids will have a place to drain out, and collect in the bandage. When doing so, you will notice that it will usually take about an hour-or-so until the blood begins to clot. At that point, you will then notice that the fluid dries out, and begins to form a scab.

*After a **FEW** hours make sure to remove the bandage.

<u>***Remember: If you choose to keep the wrap on for a while, make sure that you do not leave it on for TOO long; as you will come to find that this is actually COUNTER-PRODUCTIVE to the natural healing process (As we will discuss shortly).**</u>

WARNING: Keeping a tight wrap on your skin for more than 8+ hours, can possibly lead to skin rashes, irritation, or other localized bacterial infections.

The wrap is placed there simply to—TEMPORARILY— protect your tattoo while the natural body fluids are draining out. After that time, the natural exposure to air/oxygen is needed so as to help your skin begin to heal properly.

QUESTION: What happens if I work day-to-day in an environment where I have to deal with things such as dirt, grease, and/or other contaminants?

ANSWER: If you DO work in this type of environment, then I would recommend that you cover up your tattoo with REGULAR LOOSE-FITTING CLOTHING; rather than using a new bandage.

Once you have gotten home and removed the bandage, hop into the shower and clean off your new tattoo WELL; using an antibacterial-soap (ORGANIC if possible) and luke-warm water.

*<u>DO NOT</u> SCRUB YOUR TATTOO!

*<u>DO NOT</u> USE A WASHCLOTH OR ANYTHING ABRASIVE! BE GENTLE!

Your tattoo is not as delicate as you might think. But still, don't get all fucking crazy with it!

Wash your tattoo thoroughly! Rub over the top of it with your hand and try to remove any excess ink or dried blood/fluid/plasma/stencil-ink, etc. Be sure to remove the residue of any *Vaseline*, or any other ointments that may have been applied.

If your tattoo is larger (Or in a difficult location on the body; such as behind the knee, etc.) removing the plastic cling-film (If any was used) can be more easily done by letting it loosen up, so that it will slip-off naturally while IN the shower.

When showering, remember to keep the water temperature luke-warm—DO NOT SHOWER IN HOT WATER, HOT WATER WILL HURT!

Remember that the tattooed area is AN OPEN WOUND! A lot of people don't really realize this. Many people would describe this freshly tattooed area similar to the feeling of wrecking on a motorcycle and getting *"Road rash"*; meaning that it's like a giant scrap. If you scraped yourself, you WOULD want to wash it off. But, you would not want to put it directly under a stream of hot water (As obviously that would cause it to sting). You WOULD want to wash it off, but you would want to do so INDIRECTLY!

<u>*Remember: When showering, do not hold your tattoo DIRECTLY under the shower water, rather you will want to allow the shower water to run INDIRECTLY over your body to wash your tattoo.</u>

*Again, make sure that your shower water is not TOO hot. Hot water will not only hurt (As mentioned before) but it will also begin to create heavy amounts of steam. Steam (Like hot water), will cause your skin's pores to open up, and this may cause greater damage or loss of color/pigment.

When you were younger, your parents may have told you that after using a Jacuzzi to jump into a cold pool so as to close up your pores (As open pores can attract air-borne pathogens).

Before exiting the shower make sure to turn the temperature to ice-cold (Or as cold as you can withstand) and let the water run indirectly over your new tattoo for about 30-45 seconds. This process will help to close up the body's pores, and may also prevent any infections from any air-borne pathogens. This process will also help to prevent any further fluid drainage.

After you get out of the shower simply pat the tattooed area dry with a fresh, soft, and CLEAN cloth towel—again, the KEY-WORD here is "**GENTLY!**"

MORE ABOUT OPEN PORES

A fresh tattoo (As mentioned before), is actually an OPEN WOUND. This means that it can be subject to the possibility of an infection. But—with GOOD HYGIENE—there is really no danger of ending up with any serious infections. The problem though, is that MOST PEOPLE tend to continuously over-apply oily and petroleum-based ointments to their tattoos. Unfortunately, this is actually COUNTER-PRODUCTIVE to the tattoos natural healing process.

Now, you might think that by throwing on GOBS of ointment will make your tattoo heal faster—makes sense right? Wrong! Unfortunately, what you don't realize is that these oily/petroleum-based products will actually CLOG UP YOUR PORES and prevent your skin from breathing. Funny enough, when you do this, you are actually SUFFOCATING THE WOUND (Which will undoubtedly prolong the tattoos natural healing process). And, what's even worse is that some of these oily products have even been known to pull out minute amounts of ink/color-pigment from the skin; this can contribute to a loss of color and vibrancy in your new tattoo (More on how-to apply ointments in Section 2; please read on).

Section 2

THE FIRST WEEK

LET'S KEEP IT CLEAN!

Okay. I know, I know. Sure, this IS stating the obvious here, but again: **REMEMBER TO KEEP IT CLEAN!**—especially for AT LEAST the first few days or so.

Until your skin has transitioned through its natural healing process, you WILL need to keep a sharp eye on things! You have to remember, that your tattoo is an OPEN WOUND. Most people don't realize this, so please: **BE CAUTIOUS!**

Make sure that you keep up a conscious effort in avoiding contacting your freshly tattooed skin with any person/place/thing (Etc.) that may contain bacteria; things like letting your pet lick on your freshly tattooed skin (Pets will naturally be attracted to the odor in which the tattoo may be presenting). I've heard of this being done before, and just the mere thought of it grossed me out! People need to remember, that pets clean their own assholes with their tongues! And then they want to let that same pet's tongue lick their open wound? Why don't you just scrub some cat shit into your tattoo while you're at it? Dumb fucks… Seriously? #WTF?

Along those same lines, try not to touch your tattoo yourself; especially if you haven't washed your hands. If you're going out to the club for a drink, try not to lean your tattoo on the bar counter (If the tattoo is on your arm/elbow, etc.). During suppertime, don't go leaning your tattoo on the surface of your dining room table. If you're at work, try not to rest your tattoo on your desk. If it's date-night, and you're going out to the movies for example, don't rest your tattoo on the dirty theatre seats. If you're going out to a concert, make sure that you're not leaning up on the barricade in front of the stage. Make sure to be especially careful in watching out for germ-infested handrails leading up or down stairways, walkways, banisters, or escalator railings, etc.

TO WRAP OR RE-WRAP, THAT IS THE QUESTION

Once you've gotten home, showered up, and dried off (By patting the tattoo dry by the use of a clean and sterile towel) tattoo aftercare is relatively simple after that.

**<u>*Remember: DO NOT RE-APPLY your ALREADY USED gauze/bandage. Doing so is COMPLETELY UNSANITARY, and may also cause an infection.</u>*

*Also, **<u>DO NOT</u>** apply a NEW bandage EITHER!

Let me say that to you again, just in case you missed what I said the first time because this is so, SO important! **<u>DO NOT APPLY A NEW BANDAGE EITHER!</u>**

Applying a new bandage or gauze-wrap may possibly lead to the materials sticking to your skin—especially right after your first shower!

You will notice that as you begin to finish "Pat-drying" off your tattoo, that the tattoo will still be soft and moist. The tattoo WILL scab over in time, but right now, if you apply ANOTHER wrap on top of it, the tattoo will simply bond to the new wrap, and upon the removal of the second wrap, I can guaran-fucking-tee you (As I've seen this happen 1000x times before) that some of the color/ink will go along with it—AND IT WILL STING! The wrap will actually RIP APART your newly healing skin! If you don't follow this most important piece-of-advice (And this happens), you will then be forced to have to 1, STILL wait around another month-or-so until your tattoo heals, AND THEN 2, make yet ANOTHER APPOINTMENT with your artist in order to handle the now well-needed *touch-up* work—or as I like to call it, *"The 2nd coat."*

So, revamping on that yet again ONE MORE TIME, **DO NOT,** I repeat, **DO NOT APPLY A NEW BANDAGE!**

WHAT IN THE FUCK DO I PUT ON THIS THING?

*There is no one-single-remedy (Magic lotion, magic pill, etc.) that is used within our industry to help heal your tattoo.

Human kind has been practicing the art-of-tattooing since the dawn-of-time. There have been many scientific studies (Some even dating way back to the days of ancient cave dwelling people). Many of these studies have found reports of these pre-historic tattoo-gurus using such healing remedies on their people as aloe vera juice, and other plants that they believed may have contained healing and medicinal properties.

In actuality, a person can simply wash off their tattoo with anti-bacterial soap & water and then just leave it alone for 2-weeks. The wound WILL heal—just as any other wound does (That is what the body is naturally designed to do—heal itself); though most likely, the image may come out slightly distorted, or the color may appear to be washed out.

The purpose of PROPER aftercare, is so that we can maintain the tattoos image/structure, brightness, and color; thus helping to keep the tattoo vibrant and beautiful for many years-to-come.

Some "Artists" will advise you to just *"Keep it simple"* and, *"Just use a cotton ball and rub some rubbing alcohol over it."* The problem here, is that rubbing alcohol is designed to DRAW OUT from the wound; drawing out in this sense would mean drawing out some of the color pigment; which may cause the tattoo to end up with a dingy-like/smoky appearance, rather than one that is sharp, crisp, and vibrant. Some artists will even insist on using *Preparation H*, *Neosporin*, Cocoa Butter, *Bacitracin*, or other things of that nature—again, NOT the best idea. For example, one will find that in this industry, that many tattoo artists will—at often times—recommend (Or sometimes even INSIST) *Neosporin*. Now, one would think that *Neosporin* would heal a new tattoo rather quickly—and you're right! It will! BUT, the problem HERE, is that *Neosporin* will actually do the job TOO WELL!

I have seen many tattoos that were healed by the use of *Neosporin*. I've even used *Neosporin* myself a few times; just to see what happens. And, I must say, of all of the tattoos that I have seen (That were healed by the use of *Neosporin*) MOST had ended up with A LOT of color loss—not all of the time, but WAY too often—so beware!

Neosporin has a lot of zinc added into it, and it also contains petroleum. When *Neosporin* is applied over a fresh tattoo, it helps it to heal TOO fast; and often ends up pulling out some of the color/ink from your skin, rather than allowing your body to lock the ink in at a cellular level.

DON'T GET IT TWISTED

There are tons-and-TONS of products out there that are marketed directly for tattoo aftercare. For example, while perusing through a tattoo parlor (Or Amazon.com, or another place one may purchase tattoo supplies), one may see such products or brand names as *Tattoo Goo*, *Black Cat*, *Inkeeze*, *H2Ocean*, *Inkfix*, amongst various others. These products may LOOK good, they MAY have fancy labels on them, they may LOOK cool, and they MAY have even been seen/heard/used in many various tattoo parlors, and even television shows. BUT, the problem HERE, is that THESE PRODUCTS are really just marketing hype!

If you were to actually **READ THE INGREDIENTS** on the labels of these "Brand name" aftercare products, you would quickly come to notice that these products actually contain THE

SAME ingredients as the over-the-counter ointments (Which would actually cost you just a fraction of the price!)

Now, I may be revealing a bit too-much of the game right here, and I may even make a few enemies with the next bit-of-information that I am going to reveal to you here. But, when these items are sold in tattoo parlors by an "Artist" that recommends them, 9x times out of 10, that artist is ONLY DOING SO because he/she is actually getting paid a small amount of COMMISSION from selling that particular product!

<u>*Remember: Don't be fooled by fancy labels and/or marketing hype, READ THE INGREDIENTS on the label!</u>

Personally I use (And recommend) only one (1) product during the healing process: *Aquaphor.*

I have used *Aquaphor* before PLENTY OF TIMES on myself, and I have recommended it to clients of mine on many numerous occasions (*I am not sponsored or endorsed by *Aquaphor*, this is just MY personal recommendation to YOU THE READER).

I have personally watched many of my clients use ONLY *Aquaphor* on the tattoos that I had done on them (Applied between 1-3x times per day for approximately 10 days). All of their tattoos had turned out bright and shiny, just the way that they wanted them to, and they were all 100% satisfied.

Aquaphor is a bit thicker of a product and a little more expensive, but it's more than worth it, and it will help heal your tattoo MUCH FASTER; as it contains many healing and medicinal properties.

Now, to LOWER YOUR COST EVEN MORE—do I have your attention yet? Good! Read on.

One will find, that just as there are brand name products out there, that there are also GENERIC brands as well. *Aquaphor* has a GENERIC VERSION that is called *"Equate"*; which is sold at many different stores. *Equate* is the EXACT SAME THING as *Aquaphor*; but it is bottled in an alternate packaging. Just as there is brand name *"Vicodin"* which can be sold as its generic *"Hydrocodone"* or, brand name *"Tylenol"* which can be sold as its generic *"Acetaminophen."*

Now, if however you find that you are sensitive to *Aquaphor/Equate*-type products (As everyone's skin will have different levels of sensitivity) my second PERSONAL RECOMMENDATION would be *Lubriderm*.

Lubriderm is a smooth and creamy-like skin lotion, rather than an ointment (Which I have personally used myself on several different occasions; before I began using *Aquaphor/Equate*)

When it all comes down to it, at the end of the day, when it's all said and done, that's all you really need! *Aquaphor*, or *Lubriderm*—that's it! If you got a tattoo from me, then I know for a fact that I recommended to you one of these two products. If you decide to use something other than what I have recommended to you here, then you do so at your own risk. You do not (By-any-means) NEED to use these products in which I am recommending to you here (As you can use whatever products you like), but whichever lotion you choose to use, it should AT LEAST be DYE AND FRAGRANCE FREE (Organic if possible).

*Remember: I have spent years-and-YEARS researching tattoos and tattoo aftercare so that you don't have to. Just do yourself a favor: Try not to be a know-it-all and LISTEN TO YOUR ARTIST, otherwise you may run the risk of your tattoo not healing properly, or not coming out as bright or as vibrant as you would have liked it to do so.

DON'T RUB IT ALL IN

*Remember: All you're trying to do here, is MOISTURIZE YOUR SKIN, AND KEEP IT CLEAN! Take a small amount of *Aquaphor* or *Lubriderm* and then gently—let me say that again, GENTLY—rub it in.

You only need a thin coat of *Aquaphor.* Do not "Cake" it on, or throw on gobs and gobs. Your skin still needs to BREATHE in order to HEAL properly. You don't want to apply TOO MUCH product; as you then run the risk of suffocating the tattoo.

*Remember: You should be re-applying a thin coat of *Aquaphor* about 1-3x times daily (Dependent upon the size and/or the location of your tattoo).

*Also, if your tattoo looks dried out, then go ahead and re-apply a small amount of ointment. And again, after you shower, don't forget to **RE-APPLY IT!**

Personally, I live in the city of Las Vegas. The temperature here can reach up to 122° F! And I may have to shower up to 5x+ times per day! (Sometimes even more!) Occasionally, I will get a new tattoo from one of my fellow artists (Or perhaps even do a new one on myself). It is in fact quite common for me to be re-applying a SMALL amount of *Aquaphor* AFTER EVERY SHOWER THAT I TAKE! Some of my clients have come from different parts of the world; where many climates can vary. For example, one of my clients was from the southern-parts of the United States and he was in Las Vegas on his Summer vacation. After a bit of "Liquid-courage" my client—feeling courageous enough—had apparently mustered up the balls to FINALLY get a tattoo! And somehow managed to hit me up on my Facebook. My client was flying back home the following day to a place of utmost humidity. He had mentioned to me, that he would sometimes be forced to shower 5-10x times per day! And would still be walking around DRENCHED! (Myself, having also lived in Washington D.C., Chicago, Florida, and New York at various points in my younger life, was definitely able to relate to this predicament) I advised my client the same thing in which I have ever advised anyone else. I told him:

"Don't worry, everything will be okay. Whenever you feel the need to shower, just go ahead and wash yourself. Rinse off. Remember to pat-dry your tattoo. And simply re-apply a small bit of ointment."

*Remember: (As I said before) your tattoo is NOT as delicate as you might think that it is!

You can apply product and then shower, and then RE-apply it again as many times as needed (Though obviously THE LESS that you have to do this, the better). Hey, life isn't perfect man! Sometimes shit happens! It might get hot outside and you might need to shower off the sweat. You might be eating breakfast and then, all of a sudden… Oops! You spill your bowl of *Lucky Charms* and milk all over yourself, and you need to shower and change clothes. You might have forgot your umbrella and then come to find out that it's pouring fucking rain outside. You might try to run home, but then just end up getting soaked and need to rinse off in the shower—right after you just finished applying product! It happens! No big deal. Just re-apply more product and keep moving forward.

WHAT ABOUT THIS SPOT?

In certain areas such as your joints; the backside of your knee, the inside of your elbow, your shoulder-blades, etc. or any other area where your skin may stretch repeatedly throughout the day, tattoos can sometimes be REALLY difficult to heal.

One tattoo that I did, happened to be directly inside of my clients arm—on the crook of his elbow! My client was a health-nut and worked out in a gym at least 2x times per day! And had given me a call complaining that every time he was doing his bicep-curls that his tattoo would crack, and he didn't know whether-or-not to continually re-apply the *Aquaphor* that I had recommended to him. Now, in a perfect-world the best thing that my client could have done for his tattoo, would have been to just skip the gym for the next 2-3 weeks; until his tattoo was fully healed. But for him, that was NOT an option! So, that being the case, I had advised my client to: "Not worry about it" and to "Finish his workout routine." Upon the completion of my clients workout-routine I had advised him to "Shower up and wash over his tattoo with his hand, LIGHTLY" (So as to remove any sweat, dirt, bacteria, etc.), and then, to just simply "Apply another thin coat." After 2-weeks had passed by, my clients tattoo had healed perfectly!

If you find yourself at a point where this becomes an issue, you are most likely better off simply re-appling MORE *Aquaphor*, and keeping it slightly OVER-moisturized. But, at the same time, you may want to NOT re-apply it every time. And to instead, just go ahead and give it a few hours of *"Dry-out time"* because too much ointment will (Again) suffocate the tattoo, and could also draw out some of the color—sometimes you just can't win either way! Don't worry, it'll all be okay! That being said:

*Remember: Everyone's skin is slightly different!

Everyone—as mentioned before—will have different levels of skin sensitivity, healing time, levels of which they can take/withstand pain, and other things of that nature.

Always do what YOU think is best for YOU! But, if you have any questions: Please, don't hesitate to consult your artist IMMEDIATELY!

*Remember: No question is a dumb question! Your artist is there to HELP!

And again, if you suspect that you might be having any kind of an allergic reaction, or some other type of medical emergency, then please: Contact your doctor or physician IMMEDIATELY!

The worst thing that a person could do, would be to simply do nothing; possibly then harboring a bad situation into an even worse one. If you're confused about something, it's really best to just give someone a quick call, and get the answers in which you're seeking. Perhaps you develop a unique situation, or even some kind of serious infection? It might just be nothing, but wouldn't it be better just to check up and see? Don't be a dumb monkey! A quick-call never hurt anybody. Be smart. Be safe. This is your body, your health, and possibly even YOUR LIFE that we're talking about here!

GETTING "GEARED UP"

The first thing that you are going to want to do, is to get together some loose-fitting clothing—something that will not rub against your tattoo (Especially during the first 2-3 days of healing).

In all honesty, it's better to keep your freshly tattooed-skin exposed to the air during the healing process as much as possible. You have to remember, that ointments and lotions are greasy! If you can stay bare, all the better; as grease may STAIN your clothing!

Personally, I don't <u>EVER</u> like to cover up a new tattoo with <u>ANY</u> type of clothing! I'd rather just throw on some ointment,

RICE the-fuck-out-of-it, and just chillax out in front of my laptop watching YouTube videos. But unfortunately, I know that SOMETIMES you just don't have a choice. Sometimes bull shit just arises up out of nowhere; work, family-emergencies, special-engagements, special-events, your in-laws show up to town unannounced, etc.

One of the most uncomfortable experiences that I've ever had with tattoos, is when I've had to dress up and go to work. Being a life-coach/relationship-guru (Another business-venture of mine besides tattooing), I will usually tend to dress up wearing a suit & tie when dealing with clients. The biggest problem here, is that whatever goo that I have on me (Usually *Aquaphor*, as mentioned before) may cause the clothing over the tattoo to stick to it; which will then 1, stain my clothing with ink/grease, and 2, later on when I get home, as I try to remove the clothing, it will usually pull apart some of the scab; which can easily cause even MORE ink/color loss! To avoid this problem (Liken to the issue that I had mentioned previously within the prologue-section of this book; about the ink-stains on my sheets), I have found that washing off the ointment BEFORE covering the area with clothing (Or before bed where the tattooed area may possibly come in contact with your sheets, blankets, pillows, etc.) and just giving the tattoo some *"Dry-out"* time, will quickly eliminate this issue in its entirety—I wish my first "Artist" would have mentioned THAT one BEFORE that first issue.

You WILL tend to notice your tattoo flaking (Just a bit) as you give it some *"dry-out"* time (Just for a few hours). Seriously, it WON'T damage your tattoo! If anything, by preventing it from sticking to your clothing and your sheets, etc. it's going to heal EVEN BETTER!

*To put things into the simplest of terms: Try and avoid any type of tight-clothing that may possibly stick-to or bond-to your new tattoo. If you do have to cover that area for some time (As you are at work, etc.), just "*Go dry*" for a while. And then, re-apply your ointment once you can uncover the area.

TIME TO HIT THE SHOWERS BOYS!

You can RELAX now, showering is **ABSOLUTELY OKAY!**

Getting your tattoo wet is perfectly okay, you just don't want to SOAK the thing! Personally, I would advise you to take a normal 15-minute shower (Or as long as you would like); washing your hair and your body as you normally would. The only thing that you are going to be wanting to do differently, is that when it comes to your tattoo, try not to expose it DIRECTLY under the shower spray (As mentioned before). Also, try to shower in luke-warm water, rather that hot water; as hotter temperatures will sting your newly tattooed area!

When showering, simply wash off your tattoo with an anti-bacterial soap (*Organic if possible), and allow the shower water to rinse off the soapy area INDIRECTLY. Again, after you finish your shower, dry your tattoo off by **PATTING IT GENTLY WITH A CLEAN TOWEL!** Seriously, I cannot over emphasize this principle! **PAT IT DRY! DO NOT RUB IT!**

POOL PARTY?

Unfortunately, oceans, lakes, and rivers are FULL of bacteria, and swimming pools/Jacuzzis are full of chlorine—none of these things are really beneficial to prolonging the life of your tattoo. Just like the rules with showering, you don't want to soak your tattoo!

Saturating your tattoo with water for any great length of time is horrible! For the time being, you will want to try to avoid any such activities. Also, submerging yourself and your tattoo in the bath tub is not the best idea.

*Remember: The natural healing process only takes about 2-weeks or so. It's not really all that long! Just chill out on going swimming or hitting up the Jacuzzi for a few. Once it's finished, you can THEN go back to these types of activities. You don't want to lose color in your tattoo for the REST OF YOUR LIFE just for one day at the pool!

OTHER ACTIVITIES

Any highly-strenuous activities such as strength-training, or any contact-sports, etc. are (AGAIN) some of those things that you will just have to try and avoid for the next 2-3 weeks.

Any excessive-workouts, or any activities which would cause a person heavy-sweating are just going to have to be kept on the back-burner for the next few weeks; hot saunas, steam rooms, etc. If you are going to engage in ANY of these types of activities then please, make sure that you take the proper precautions beforehand!

*TIP: The best thing that you can do, is to just try to get a bit of R&R (Rest & Relaxation). You have your whole life ahead of you to do whatever you want! Take a little time off to allow your tattoo—a thing that is going to be with you **FOR THE REST OF YOUR LIFE**—to heal **PROPERLY!**

CATCHIN' SOME ZZZs

If you remember back in the prologue-section of this book, I had mentioned the issue of what happens if you go to bed while STILL covered in ointment—it can be VERY messy, so beware!

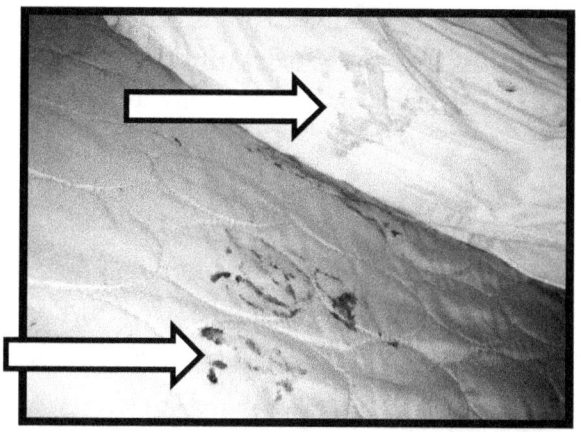

Above: A clients bedding (Sheets, pillows, and comforter) that was recently ruined because he'd chosen not to listen to the advice in which I had given him on showering off any product that he was wearing before bed, and "Going dry."

When it comes to sleeping, I have one general routine that I tend to follow religiously, and that is: To shower off before bed (Removing any ointment), pat the tattoo **DRY** (Not still damp, not soft, but **DRY!**), and then, try as best that I can to **NOT SLEEP DIRECTLY ON THE TATTOOED AREA!** When I wake up- (First thing in the late-afternoon, or possibly even the early-evening—remember I'm not a morning person ;) -I will then re-apply my ointment before starting my day.

Some artists have suggested that sprinkling baby powder onto your sheets before bed will help to protect your tattoo, but personally, I wouldn't recommend it—just *go dry*! It's easier, and perfectly safe.

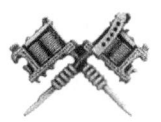

Another thing that you will find, is that upon waking up, your tattoo (After about a weeks-time) will begin looking dry, and may appear as if it is cracking.

You may notice in your bed small white flakes; like that of dandruff or dried skin. Don't worry, this is just another stage in the healing process.

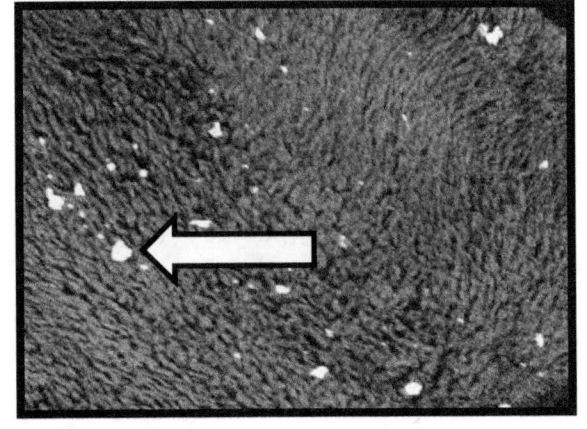

If you happen to wake up and see these small flakes of dried skin in your bed, just use it as a quick morning reminder (After you get up and get showered) to put on some ointment. As said before, it's good to *go dry* FOR A WHILE, but not TOO LONG! You've slept, now grease-up and go about your business.

"TAT SHEETS"

Now, you WILL sweat throughout the night; that's just a fact of life. What this means, is that YOU WILL lose a minute amount of ink REGARDLESS! But, you can prevent any loss/damage to your "Good" set of sheets by simply buying a special-set of *"Tat sheets."*

If you are going to be getting A LOT of ink-work done, then it may be in your best interest to purchase an extra set of black sheets for use while your tattoos are still in the healing process. You can buy a pair of black sheets from Wal-Mart for under $7—a VERY wise investment! Once your tattoo is healed, simply wash, dry, and fold up your *tat sheets*, and then store them in your linen-closet until your next session.

CATCHIN' SOME RAYS

Hmmm, yeah… Can we say "OUCH!"

One of the reasons I may cover up a client's tattoo after he leaves, is to stop its exposure to direct sunlight.

Direct sunlight is HORRIBLE for your new tattoo! And for your already healed ones as well! I've walked outside myself after just getting inked up; just to see what it was like—yeah... Not the business! The sunlight WILL sting/burn the tattooed area!

If you tend to spend a lot of your time out in the sun, over time, your tattoo WILL begin to fade; not within a weeks-time, but over the course of the next few years. To keep your tattoos looking THEIR BEST, try and keep out of direct sunlight and/or prolonged exposure to the sun (More on prolonging the life of your tattoo later).

SUNSCREEN

Personally, I would never recommend the use of ANY sunscreen or sunblock! Most people are unaware that it is actually sun<u>SCREEN</u> that causes skin-cancer, not the sun itself—READ THE INGREDIENTS! Sunscreens are full of toxic poisons! It is a scam!

Sunscreen MAY help to prevent a sun-burn TODAY, but it may cause MANY skin problems down the road! But, for the time being, using sunscreen in <u>minute amounts</u> while your tattoo is healing—if you must be out in the sun—is DEFINITELY a good idea!

Personally, I live in Las Vegas. The climate here is direct sunlight—sometimes in excess of 120° F—throughout most of the year, and I NEVER use sunscreen.

SCABBING, PEELING, AND FLAKING

Do not PICK at your new tattoo! Let me say that again, **DO NOT**—can you hear me clearly?—**PICK... AT... YOUR NEW TATTOO!!!**

You will begin to notice (After about 2-3 days or so) that during the natural healing process the scab will begin to start shedding—this is perfectly normal! You will also begin to notice, that the tattooed-area may begin to feel a bit itchy. The advice here: **DON'T PICK!**—And don't fuckin' scratch it either!

If your skin itches, then simply <u>PAT it</u>—**GENTLY!** Some artists will insist that you "Slap it"—again, not really the best idea. Other artists have suggested applying a bit of rubbing alcohol, or other alcohol-based products (I.e.-*Listerine*, *Scope*, *Bactine*, etc.), in order to help temporarily relieve the itching/irritation—personally, I wouldn't. Again, just pat the area a bit! I know it's annoying, but your tattoo will be healed soon enough, and then you can scratch that area to your heart's content!

<u>*Remember: If you notice that your skin is peeling, then you NEED to apply more *Aquaphor*/*Lubriderm*/lotion, etc., on it!</u>

HEAVY SCABBING

As mentioned before, there are certain areas of the body, which may—despite your best efforts—end up with SOME amount of heavy/heavier scabbing (For example, on the crook of your elbow/knee/shoulder-blades, etc.).

The constant movements of your body (Rubbing/friction, etc.) within these types of areas, can make it EXCEEDINGLY more difficult for the tattooed-skin to heal up properly! At first, you MAY end up with some heavy scabbing (Though only for a time). It WILL heal eventually, so don't worry.

One particular case I had witnessed, was after I'd worked on a client's leg-tattoo. My client had later returned to show me his leg (Which was completely scabbed over), and he was asking my advice as to what he should do (*My client had ALSO admitted to me that he was not "Regularly" applying the *Aquaphor* in which I had recommended to him either).

I first had my client lift up his pants-leg; so as to give his heavily-scabbed area a quick look-see. I didn't notice any redness or swelling present, and to the best of my knowledge I had concluded that the area wasn't in fact infected. I then advised him go home and HYDRATE the area in a warm bath (*Another exception to the rules—though for only a very short period of time; 10-15 minutes MAXIMUM!), and to then (Afterwards), pat the tattoo down with a clean towel, and to apply a thicker coat of *Aquaphor*.

In performing this action, my client was quickly able to soften the hard scab that had formed over his tattoo; thereby causing some of the scab's harder outer-layers to wear away (Thinning the scab out—just a bit—whilst still preventing much color loss).

Now, here's the kicker: Had this process been done in ANY other way (I.e., soaking the tattoo and then pealing it off, etc.), it may have resulted in not only a loss of color pigment, but may also have been quite painful; and quite possibly could have even lead to permanent scarring! Ironically enough, sometimes the REMOVAL of some of this heavy scabbing will actually result in an overall better healing for the rest of the tattoo.

Worst-case-scenario, when dealing with heavy scabbing, is that you MAY (If you notice after the tattoo is FULLY healed that there has been a significant amount of color loss) need to call up your artist; so as to set up a 2nd appointment; so that he/she can go back and do some *"Touch-up"* work. Or, as I said before: What I like to refer to as, *"The 2nd coat."*

REDNESS & SWELLING

You may feel as if your tattoo—or the area SURROUNDING your tattoo—is sore. It may feel heavy. You might visibly see a bit of redness and/or swelling. The area might burn or sting a bit. It might feel as if someone hit you—or physically PUNCHED you in that area! It may feel sore; similar in the fashion as when your muscles become sore after an extensive-workout at the gym. It may even throb a bit! Don't worry! All of these symptoms are completely NORMAL!

If you notice an extensive-level of redness around your tattoo, or the tattooed area, it does not mean—IN ANY WAY WHAT-SO-EVER—that your tattoo is "Infected!" You **DO NOT** have to rush off to the emergency room—relax!

I've had a couple of first-time clients call me up 2-3 days after getting tattooed complaining that their tattoo was quote-on-quote "Infected", and were wondering whether-or-not they should go to the E.R.—The answer is "NO!" Just RELAX! The redness that you are seeing is part of the skin's natural healing process. What you are seeing is an excess-amount of blood that has risen up towards the surface area. It is NEEDED in order to help begin healing up the open wound.

RUBBING ALCOHOL

If you want to tone down the redness just a bit—just for your own personal piece-of-mind—you CAN rub some rubbing alcohol on the tattooed-area using a cotton-ball. This will usually tone down the redness, and will also kill off any bacteria. Do keep in mind though, that when performing this technique, that rubbing alcohol is designed to PULL/DRAW OUT things from a wound; which can possibly lead to permanent ink-damage and/or color loss.

A few people that I know, who are really into tattoos, and who had used this rubbing alcohol technique in the past, have admitted to me, that their tattoos had ended up slightly faded. I have even experimented with rubbing alcohol myself! After my tattoos had fully-healed, I would describe them as having a "*Smoked*" or "*Dingy*-like" appearance. Lucky for me, I was able to just call up a fellow artist and have him touch it up for me—as fellow artists will commonly do for one-and-other within this industry. For regular people though, to fix THIS ISSUE could possibly cost them $100s of dollars! That being the case, I would advise AGAINST using rubbing alcohol during the healing process of your tattoo.

BRUISING

If you begin to notice a bit of bruising or discoloration (Colors such as blue, black, purple, yellow, green, etc.), again, remember: This is PERFECTLY NORMAL!

Every person's skin has a different levels of sensitivity. Some people just bruise easier than others! Sometimes, bruising (In this fashion) MAY take some time to heal. For some people, it may take an entire month to heal! While others, it may take up to 3+ months! And sometimes, possibly even longer! Now, if however 6+ months have passed by, and your tattoo STILL looks as if it is discolored or darker in appearance around the area where the lines SHOULD have stopped, this is what is known as being *"Blown out"* or, *"The lines are blown out."* What happened here, is that your tattoo artist was not tattooing that particular point of the tattoo at the correct angle. Unfortunately, there is no way to fix this problem; except by tattooing SOMETHING ELSE over the top of that area. For example, you may want to *"Smoke it out"* or add *"Clouds"*, or something similar of that nature using a *"Grey wash."*

Most likely, in order to fix this particular issue (As some people are perfectionists—and it is YOUR BODY; so in which you DO have a right to be), you may just have to add something BIG and BLACK over the top of the blown-out area; so as to cover it up.

Hopefully not a cock—unless you're into that sort of thing. And... Well... If that's the case: Then hey! Do your thang player!

ICING YOUR TATTOO

If it really is just a bit of bruising, then you are more than welcome to simply ICE your tattoo; in order to try and reduce some of the swelling.

To ice your tattoo, simply use a cold press, an ice pack, or even just a *Zip-Lock* bag full of ice cubes (And/or frozen fruits/vegetables), and water—you can even use and ice-cold can of beer! And hold it on top of the bruised/swollen area.

<u>*Remember: When icing your tattoo (Or ANY other bump, bruise, swollen area, etc.) to ONLY DO SO IN 5-15 MINUTE INCREMENTS!</u>

This means that you will want to ICE IT FOR 5-15 MINUTES, and then LEAVE IT ALONE FOR 5-15 MINUTES, and then repeat. You are more-than-welcome to do this process as many times as needed until you either feel more comfortable, or until the swelling resides.

ELEVATION

Another thing that may help you to relieve the swelling, is to ELEVATE your tattoo. For example: If the tattoo is on your leg, then simply lay down on the couch and prop up your leg with a pillow as you ice it (Also see RICE). You may even want to take some pain-relief medications, or some anti-inflammatories.

RICE: REST, ICE, COMPRESS, ELEVATE

The acronym *RICE* is so, SO important! *RICE* is an acronym for Rest, Ice, Compress, Elevate. To "*RICE*" your tattoo, you do simply that: Rest, ice, compress, and elevate. You can *RICE* your tattoo at any time throughout the healing process; it will not damage it what-so-ever!

Personally, I like to *RICE* my tattoos; mostly during the first 2-3 days. That is the time-frame where your new tattoo will be the most swollen, and/or the most painful!

When I *RICE* my tattoos, I like to use an ice pack (You can easily purchase one at *Wal-Mart* for under $2 dollars). After I have my ice pack, I then set out for myself a platter of ice cream, potato chips, or any other types of snack foods that I'm in the mood for—possibly even a 6-pack of beer—maybe more! Load myself up a phat bowl of chronic in my water bong. And then, just veg-out on the couch for a few hours while watching *YouTube* video-playlists of my favorite posted material.

INFECTIONS

Eww… Gross!

Infections—oddly enough—are the last thing in which we are going to discuss in THIS section; but the topic is DEFINITELY one of UTMOST importance!

While infections are actually not very common, they ARE still however a POSSIBILITY—and you DO need to be knowledgeable of them.

When we talk about infections, we are not just talking about a bit of bacteria on a needle that has ended up there because the artist forgot to wash his/her hands. When we're talking about infections, WE—as professionals—are more so referring to things such as HIV/AIDS, Hepatitis, MRSA, Staph infections, Mycobacterium, Haemophilum/Chelonae, and other things liken to THAT nature.

Sometimes (Even the most skilled artists) can end up *"Sticking"* themselves with the needle by accident. Gloves CAN provide SOME protection, but I have personally seen one artist I had been working with *stick* himself while he was tattooing me— sometimes freak-accidents just happen to occur!

For example, one time while in a shop, a young man BURST through the front door and shouted out:

"WHADDUP DAWG!"

This action startled my artist; as he was *"In the zone"*, and there was no prior warning. My artist then—whilst in the midst of tattooing—recoiled his right hand (Which was holding the gun) causing him to poke himself with the needle on his opposite forearm—OUCH! Now personally, I don't have anything—but HE doesn't fuckin' know that! After that, my artist was forced to change the needle that he was using—but what if he didn't? What if he just decided to not say anything, and had just continued tattooing me? Would I have ever known the difference? Probably not—but what if HE had something? What if he had AIDS? It's the little things like these that can be so, SO dangerous, because these are the types of things that can happen in the world of tattooing.

So, how can you tell if your tattoo is infected? Well, some key signals that a tattoo may be infected, could be a reddish-color surrounding the tattooed-area for any extensive amount of time (*Not the first 2-3 days but if you still notice that the area is REALLY RED days-and-days later—yeah, you might have a problem). You may notice a bit (Or an excessive amount) of yellow or green puss that is oozing outwards from the area. You may notice a funny odor or a foul scent. You may notice that if you were to touch the area, that it would be excessively more warm; possibly even HOT (Liken to the experience of touching someone's forehead while they have a fever). You may notice excessive swelling or discoloration. You may suffer excessive pain. You may become sick, or experience any multitude of other signs/symptoms, etc. (***REMEMBER: THIS IS NOT A MEDICAL GUIDE!** This is a guide on TATTOO AFTERCARE! If you notice any of these types of signs/symptoms then please: **CONTACT YOUR DOCTOR OR PHYSICIAN IMMEDIATELY!!!**)

Try to keep in mind, if you do suffer from an infection, that it may not be entirely your fault! It IS possible for you—AS WELL AS YOUR TATTOO ARTIST—to do everything PERFECTLY, and you may STILL end up with an infection!—That's just life! And—as many of us artists will agree—sometimes, it's just part of the whole tattooing experience.

If you do end up getting an infection, it's not the end of the world. At the end of the day, all we can really do is to be as safe, and as clean, and as professional as we can, in order to help prevent ANY of these types of issues from occurring.

RED DYE REACTION

There is a small percentage of people who do end up with something called *"Red Dye Reaction"*—usually people who have a very high-level of skin-sensitivity.

If you are one of those types of people who find that they are usually allergic to cheap metal-jewelry, or other things of that nature, this can be an early warning-sign for a potential future problem.

Cheap metal (Such as fake/faux gold chains) are usually crafted with an excessive amount of nickel in them. Many red tattoo-inks have nickel in them as well, and sometimes the red-ink will not heal very easily. If you feel that you might have a nickel allergy then please, let your artist know as soon as possible so as to take the proper precautions.

To avoid this problem early on, you may want to either: 1, choose a different colored ink for that area, or 2, just try to find an organic substitute ink that is "Nickel free."

Just as many conventional foods use chemicals such as *Red Dye #5* or *Red Dye #40* to give things such as peppermint its bright red color, ORGANIC foods will typically use organic fruit and/or vegetable juices for color, which is obviously MUCH healthier for you

In general, anything ORGANIC is usually going to be better for your overall health & wellness, and will also be safer for either consumption, or for use to put in your skin.

Feel free to do a very small *"Test spot"* and then wait to finish your tattoo until it has fully healed. You can always tattoo over the top of your test spot with a darker colored ink if your skin doesn't take the red.

Section 3

PROLONGING THE LIFE
OF YOUR TATTOO

RE-APPLYING PRODUCT

After your tattoo has FULLY-healed, if you're REALLY worried about the color of your tattoo, then feel free to apply a bit of product every few weeks or so—possibly even every couple of months.

I have known some clients to be VERY picky about their work. People have mentioned to me—on numerous occasions—that they will typically (Just as part of their everyday regime) apply just a "Bit" of product—obviously this is NOT necessary.

Now, if you're going to be out-and-about in the hot sun on any particular day, then guess what? IT STILL DOESN'T MATTER! It's just ONE day! But, if you (For example) work construction, and are on a job-site that is outside in a place where the sun will be in direct contact with your tattoo for 8-12+ hours of the day, for a period of 6+ months or so, then YES! You may want to use some of the techniques we spoke about earlier in the section on sunscreen.

If you don't want to use sunscreen, or don't want to have to deal with putting on product and enduring the mess/greasiness of it on your skin, then just go ahead and put on a layer of clothing over the top of it; so as to cover it up.

WEIGHT GAIN/WEIGHT LOSS

A few things to keep in mind when getting a tattoo, is to take into consideration whether-or-not you will be either gaining or losing weight.

Personally, I have never noticed a person's tattoos to change all that much due to either gaining or losing weight. I was 220+ lbs myself at one point! And have since lost over 70+ lbs! And I have never noticed any significant difference in the appearance of ANY of my tattoos. I have however seen a girl get pregnant who had recently gotten a tattoo on her stomach area. As she moved through her pregnancy, her tattoo did stretch quite a bit. After she had delivered the baby, she did hit the *Stair-Master* HARD, and managed to lose the weight she had put on; but she did end up getting a few stretch-marks. The stretch-marks had ruined part of her tattoo, the color was just gone; leaving the tattoo broken-like in appearance. This is just something to be aware of, because again, life happens.

WHAT ABOUT STRENGTH-TRAINING?

In regards to strength training, unless you're at a point where TODAY your under -100 lbs, and you plan on becoming Arnold Schwarzeneggr and putting on 200+ lbs of pure lean muscle.

Then you really have nothing to worry about. Lift weights, grow strong, relax, have fun. You won't damage or stretch-out your tattoo.

WHAT IF I GET FAT?

Life happens. Sometimes we get older. We gain weight. Our metabolism changes—shit happens.

I would recommend to you, to try and stay as fit, and as healthy as you can. Live a life of proper diet & nutrition, and try to always stay active.

I know sometimes we all get stuck at the office, and only have 30 minutes to break, and all that's nearby is a fuckin' Micky Deez—it happens! Your tattoo isn't going to stretch out unless you end up adding on like 200+ lbs or so.

Fat does not ALL store in one single area. When your body stores fat it is spread out all over your body bit-by-bit. If you end up gaining 20-30 lbs or so, don't worry about it, instead just hit the track; not necessarily for your tattoo's shape, but rather for your general health, and well-being.

LET'S "MAKE IT POP!"

Personally, I have a bright red lipstick-kiss tattoo on the right side of my neck. Some people get these types of tattoos for their wives or girlfriends. I got mine more-so like a medal/trophy for my side-business (I have a side-business where I teach guys how to pick-up women—like the movie *"Hitch"* starring Will Smith except 1000x times more aggressive).

I was recently featured on the covers of two big magazines here in Las Vegas; Las Vegas' *SEVEN* & *CITY LIFE* magazines. And went on a 22-city tour across America, where I was able to help 1000s of single men and women with dating and relationship advice. Along the way (Using MY OWN top-secret tips & techniques) I had also picked-up 100s of women myself! So, all-in-all, my lipstick-kiss tattoo is really there as the mark of a REAL player in the game—straight up!

Now, before I go out I like to *"Make it pop"* by applying a very small amount of *Aquaphor* or *Vaseline* so that it REALLY stands out!

This technique is really fun to do when I'm going out to the club! When using this technique inside of a dark night club a person cannot distinguish the difference whether-or-not the lipstick-kiss is real. Girls will walk up and point at my bright-red tattoo and will say, "OMG! Haha! Whose lips are those?" To which I will reply, "Oh man! It's Vegas, haha! There's BIG mosquitos out here this time of year" (Ending the sentence with a wink and spoken in a very flirty and playful-like fashion). Upon delivering my *canned* response (In which I call *"Intro-skripting"*) the girls will quickly explode into laughter. It's a great ice-breaker, and it will usually spark up a fun and interesting conversation thereafterwards. Other times they may just ask me, "Who kissed you right there?" To which I will quickly cut them off and reply, "Yeah, but she only got ONE SIDE! What's up with that?" The girl will laugh and say "Yeah, I know right?" To which I will then reply (As I point FIRMLY at the OTHER SIDE of my neck, "Make me match on THIS side!" And then, just like that, the girl will lean over and give me a REAL lipstick-kiss on the other side of my neck!—And after that happens… Well… Hey, what happens in Vegas… You know the rest! (Well, actually THESE DAYS anything that happens in Vegas usually just ends up on Facebook! ;)

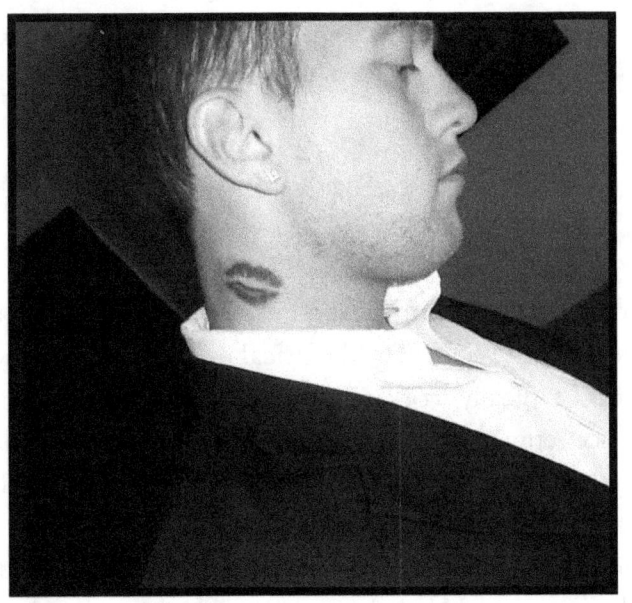

If you have a tattoo and you want to *"Make it pop"*, simply smear on a small sheen of *Aquaphor* or *Vaseline*.

*Remember: You CAN use *Vaseline* NOW at this point because THIS technique is NOT part of the healing process. THIS technique is done only AFTER your tattoo is FULLY-healed).

UV PROTECTION

As mentioned numerous times before, if you're going to be out in the sun for any elongated amount of time, then you should try to provide SOME level of protection (Not for just 1-day, but for an extended period of time; 3-6+ months of HEAVY exposure daily).

IS ALL THIS UV PROTECTION STUFF REALLY ALL THAT NECESSARY?

Well, here's the REAL DEAL. I live out in Las Vegas; a place most plentiful with direct sunlight—sometimes in excess of 120° degrees!

By trade (Besides my music, and my lifestyle/dating coaching businesses), I'm a recording/theatrical engineer. I work with bands, and I typically work outside in a concert/festival-type setting—sometimes in excess of 16+hours a day! I've done residency-tours with Guns 'N' Roses, Def Leppard, Motley Crüe, KISS, Carlos Santana, Tiësto, and 100s of other major international musical acts. Some of these concerts are indoors, while others are outside in the hot sun! The truth is: I have NEVER ONCE applied ANY sunscreen, or ANY other form of protection, and I have never once noticed that ANY of my tattoos have faded. Oh… And did I ALSO mention that I commute back-and-forth to work in a convertible? (That's how we roll in the west) Yeah. I get A LOT of sun exposure to my tattoos—never had a problem though.

Now, for safety's sake, and just for precautionary measures, SURE, go ahead and apply some product if it will give you some peace-of-mind, but it really isn't all that necessary. I've proved it, friends of mine have proved it, but if you feel safer in doing so, then by-all-means, go for it! No one is going to judge you otherwise. But, on the real though: Once your tattoo has fully-healed, that is most-likely how it's going to stay looking for some time.

THE WHEEL IN THE SKY KEEPS ON TURNING

The oldest tattoos that I have on me now, are well over 15-years-old, and they are still as dark as they were a month after I had first got them!

I have friends in their late 40s, and even 50s and 60s, who had all gotten tattoos back when they were in their early teens and 20s. Some of their tattoos have faded, just slightly. Others, a lot. While others, not much at all.

*Remember: EVERYONE'S SKIN IS DIFFERENT!

Do the best that you can do to take good care of your tattoo! And, as mentioned (Now numerous times before) don't worry too much. Your tattoo is not as delicate as you might think that it is, so just relax!

LIFE AFTER DEATH

Most people have the mindset of: *"I'll have it for the rest of my life"* or, *"I'll have it until the day that I die."* Which is true in a sense, but interesting enough, your tattoo doesn't just magically disappear at the moment of your death.

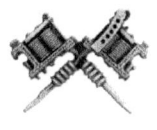

Science has now discovered that your tattoo will actually stay on your body EVEN AFTER YOUR DEATH! Crazy right?

Your tattoos will stay on your body until your skin decomposes; which can take 6+ months (Or even longer) depending upon how well your body was preserved—just something interesting to keep in mind. Your family can have it removed if they like, but it is rather expensive.

<u>*Remember: That tattoo that you just put on last week is going to be around EVEN LONGER THAN YOU!</u>

ETERNALLY INKED

Even weirder than the last section, there is now also a new movement being created by a private organization in Europe, which allows family members of the deceased, the option to have the corpse's tattooed skin removed from the body, and then (While packaged in formaldehyde) be shipped over to a special lab where pathologists will extract the water and fat cells, and replace it with a liquid polymer; typically silicon. This process basically turns the tattooed-skin into a plastic-like object; thus preserving it—indefinitely.

Now, in the same fashion that some families choose to cremate a person's body and keep their ashes stored in an urn on the mantle above the fireplace, they can now ALSO keep an ACTUAL PIECE of the person. The process is rather expensive, but it is being done; meaning that: The tattoo that you get today, could possibly become IMMORTALIZED—just something to think about.

Section 4
FINAL THOUGHTS

MY "FRIEND"

Many clients have come to tell me, "My FRIEND told me to do… (Blank)" or, "My FRIEND told me that I should do… (Such-and-such)"—I hear this ALL THE TIME. At this point, I have to then advise my clients and ask them questions such as, "Has your FRIEND had years-and-years of experience in this field?" Or, "Has your FRIEND dealt with 100s of clients, and/or done 100s of tattoos on different people?" Or, "Has your FRIEND had over 60+ tattoos on his OWN body, and learned/studied/or ever wrote the book on proper tattoo aftercare?" Hmmm, let me think about that… Probably not! That being the case: DO NOT LISTEN TO "YOUR FRIEND."

In life, you should always **LISTEN TO THE PEOPLE WHO HAVE WHAT YOU WANT**! Listen to your ME, Listen to YOUR ARTIST, listen to other PROFESSIONALS within the industry—DO NOT LISTEN TO "YOUR FRIEND!"

*Remember: If you feel something is wrong then please, PLEASE REACH-OUT-TO-YOUR-ARTIST!!!

Again, everyone's skin is going to be different. Every person has different antibodies running through them. One person my take a certain color ink while another person's body may simply reject that color all together! Some people bleed more than others. Some people are more sensitive to pain. Etc., etc., etc., etc., ETC.! Again, this is just MY ADVICE. This is advice that I myself have used that has helped my tattoos stay bright, vibrant, and colorful, and has helped myself (Along with many of my clients) stay happy, healthy, and satisfied with their new tattoos.

Please, have common-sense, and follow the advice in which I have given to you here. And, if you have any questions, please feel free to call either myself, or your artist.

*Remember: There is no such thing as a "Dumb question." If you don't know—THEN FUCKING ASK! It really is in your best interest to do so. You don't want to end up with something such as blood poisoning, bacteremia, septicemia, or any other type of nasty infection, or something else of that nature.

IN CLOSING

I want to thank you so much for taking the time to read this material. By doing so, you are a huge step closer to healing your new tattoo PROPERLY.

*Remember: This is YOUR BODY that we're talking about here. This tattoo is going to be on you for the REST OF YOUR LIFE!

A NEW AGE OF TATTOOING

With prices so affordable now, doing ink-work is beginning to become much more common; more-so than at any other time in human history! Kids as young as 9 and 10-years-old can now simply use their parents credit-card, order a machine, ink, and a pack of needles from online-stores such as *Amazon.com* (Or various others) and sit around after school and draw on each other—PERMANENTLY! (For a little as under $10!)

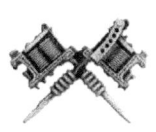

Being a music artist, I'm very heavily involved with things such as social media; *Facebook*, *Instagram*, *Twitter*, *Tumblr*, etc. Being that I do rap and other various forms of pop-music, I deal with most of my fans being between the ages of 7-19-ish. I have seen *Instagram* pictures of two 13-year-old boys on my "Followers list" who are working on *sleeving* each other up; they post new pics on my *Instagram* regularly, and will occasionally DM me (Direct Message) questions/comments/inquiries, etc. on how they can better take care of their tattoos—this happens guys, this is real life!

We live in the real world here people! I'm not here to tell anyone what they can or can't do with their lives. This is YOUR BODY! No one has the right to tell YOU what you can or cannot put on it, or into it; or anything thing else like that! But, I do advise any of you doing so TO REALLY THINK ABOUT WHAT YOU'RE DOING BECAUSE <u>TATTOOS ARE FOR LIFE</u>!

<u>*Remember: Be CONSCIOUS of things, and TAKE GOOD CARE OF YOUR NEW TATTOO AFTER IT'S FINISHED!</u>

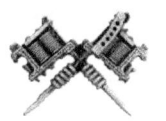

I was recently hanging out at a tattooing session with Albert. It was in the early morning—I was still up from partying the night before with my homegurl. I needed him to do a bit of touch-up work on a tattoo that I had gotten from another artist prior to working with him. Albert had 2 clients that morning; a 60-year-old man, and a 16-year-old girl (Who had arrived there early with her mother; so as to give Albert her parental consent). Later on that same week, I was clothes-shopping at the mall, and out of the corner of my eye I had noticed a very young girl, who—interestingly enough—had 2 stars tattooed on her FACE, right next to her left eye.

I was quite intrigued. The stars looked great—very professionally done (In-my-opinion), but she was so young looking.

Interesting... I thought.

I had to find out what had inspired this girl to get a PERMANENT MARK on her FACE at such a very young age.

A few kids that I had known back in high school had managed to get a random artist who worked in a shop on the Venice Beach Boardwalk to tat them up at 16, but their tattoos were underneath their clothes. This tattoo was on the girls FACE!

"That's a bold statement!" I said as I pointed towards the young girls tattooed stars on her face, "Those look tight. Who did those?"

"Oh, haha! I got these last year when I was 13. My friend from school did them" She told me.

"Hell yeah, that's what's up!" I replied.

The point that I'm trying to make here, is that EVERYONE is getting tattooed these days—people of all ages; men, women, boys, girls, doctors, lawyers, etc.—it's all just part of pop-culture now.

So, like it or not, tattoos are here to stay! I just want you—whoever you are—to remember to take good care of YOURS! Go ahead and take that extra few minutes this morning to REALLY MAKE YOURS SHINE, and GET THE MOST OUT OF IT! Let's make um shine. Or better yet, Let's *"make um POP!"* ;)

TO THE LIFE OF YOUR TATTOO

Okay guys, this is Ryan Jaunzemis signing off. I want to personally thank you for purchasing my product, and I hope that this book has brought you a few new insights. I hope my advice will assist you in the natural healing process of your new tattoo. I wish you Godspeed, and a quick and safe recovery.

For more advice on tattoos and tattoo aftercare make sure to visit my new website www.TattoosByRyanJaunzemis.com

For your health, and for the life of your tattoo, this is Ryan Jaunzemis.

Thank you, & best wishes to you all,

Ryan Jaunzemis
www.TattoosByRyanJaunzemis.com | 702.417.7714

About The Author
RYAN JAUNZEMIS

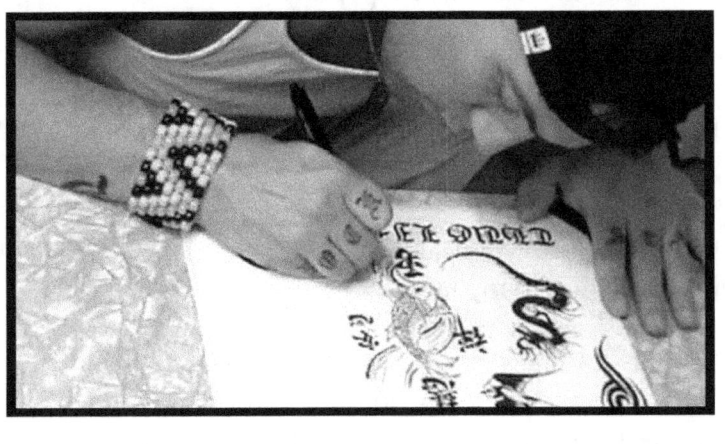

Ryan Christopher Jaunzemis (Born February 5, 1980 in Inglewood, California), also known as "Ryan Jay" by many of his fans, is an American virtuoso—a rapper, singer/song-writer, executive-producer/director, pro skater, author, lifestyle, dating, & relationship/self-help guru, internet marketer, photographer/videographer, graphic designer, tattoo artist, black-belt/martial-arts master, and recording/theatrical engineer. Ryan currently resides in Las Vegas, Nevada.

BEGINNINGS IN TATTOOING

The first tattoo that I ever did was for a friend back in 2006 with a gun that I had fashioned out of a black *Bic*-pen, a guitar E-string, and a small motor that I had extracted out of a clock-radio. We were on a lot of different drugs at the time, and it just seemed like a pretty fun thing to do on that particular evening. Funny enough, I felt pretty comfortable and at home throughout the entire process, and the tattoo came out relatively decent— even with the jail-house-type equipment.

My friend admired his new tattoo, and had told me:

"Damn dawg! I think you might have found your niche."

Ever since then, I have done tattoos for friends & family out of my house; nothing serious, just for fun, as I have other business ventures going on in my life.

Personally, I think every group of friends should have SOMEONE on their crew who does tattoos, as 1, it's more intimate and personal—almost tribal-like, and 2, I've heard it can be wayyyyy cheaper than paying some of the outrageous shop-prices—especially here in Vegas.

TATTOOING CAREER

Tattoos By Ryan Jaunzemis, author of the book/audio-book **"TATTOO AFTERCARE**—*The Full-Guide For The Freshly Inked.*"

TATTOOING STYLE

Urban/gangsta (Skript writing, flash, tribal, black-work, etc.).

RYAN JAUNZEMIS IN POPULAR CULTURE

Ryan Jaunzemis, pro skater, has been featured in *Soap Shoes'* **national and international sales commercials,** *Relate Video Productions* famous full-length Soap videos "*ONE*" & "*TWO*", and has been rated "*The best Soaper in the world*" by www.Soapshoe.com. Ryan is also the author of the book "**SOAP SHOES — Secret Tips & Tricks**" and, "**THE NEW SOAP SHOES TRICKTIONARY** (*Version 2.0*)"

BUSINESS VENTURES

Ryan Jaunzemis Music, Ryan Jaunzemis Lifestyle Coaching, Jaunzemis Entertainment, Tattoos By Ryan Jaunzemis, and many others.

HONORS

Ryan Jaunzemis, world renowned lifestyle & dating guru, has recently been featured on the covers of Las Vegas' *SEVEN* & *CITY LIFE* Magazines, *Her Obsession* **Magazine,** and *PUALingo.com.* Ryan helps men and women—the world over—to achieve better success with relationships, with business, and with life. Ryan is best known for his new underground DVD documentary "**THE LAS VEGAS LAIR**—*The Mini-Movie*" (A new full-length film on Las Vegas' *PUA & Seduction Community,* and is the author of the book "*REAL GAME*", as well as several other publications.

Contact Information

Ryan Jaunzemis | 702.417.7714
(Videochat available; *FaceTime*, *Skype*, *ooVoo*, *Tango*, etc.)

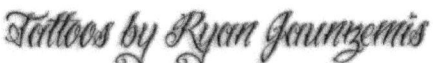

www.TattoosByRyanJaunzemis.com

www.Facebook.com/RyanJaunzemisTattooPage

www.Instagram.com/Jaunzemis | @jaunzemis

www.Twitter.com/RyanJaunzemis

www.RyanJaunzemis.Tumblr

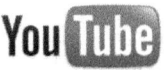

www.YouTube.com/TheRyanJayShow

Notes